BILL NEWMAN

HOW TO AVOID DETOURS ON

THE ROAD TO SUCCESS

KEYS TO HELP YOU CONQUER

THE 10 MOST COMMON

CAUSES OF FAILURE

How to avoid detours on the road to success

BILL NEWMAN INTERNATIONAL

I.S.B.N. 1 875121 18 8

©1995 BILL NEWMAN
ALL RIGHTS RESERVED
PUBLISHED BY
BILL NEWMAN CRUSADES
P.O. BOX 195
TOOWONG, QLD 4066
AUSTRALIA
TEL +61 (0)7 3371 0750 , FAX +61 (0)7 3870 1664

Each of us travels our road in life, hoping it will be the road to success. In this book, Bill makes sure we know how to make our road, the road to success. Bill Newman shows the reader, not only how to avoid detours, but what the detours are. This is a "must read book' for the person who wants to get the most out of his life by teaching him how to make the most of his life.

...Terri Gulick

What a book! Bill has given us an extremely practical and straightforward guide in how to improve ourselves and, at the same time, avoid many of the common pitfalls. It is a book for every person who has ambition.

... Tom Avelsgaard

"You've done it again, Bill - straight to the point, always optimistic, sprinkling the truth with fun.
I love the way you make each paragraph a new story or a fresh truth; they are like windows letting in light, making them obvious and relative.
Thanks for helping me to see more of myself, face myself and change my habits, Bill. Tomorrow will be better for it."

...Winston Broad

I want you to know that this book is just plain great. The straightforward simplicity of power phrases should be adopted by all that truly want to build a life. I say - read it, apply it and enjoy the fruit. I use the book all the time for seminars and marketing.

...Tony Renard

As we pursue our destiny and purpose in life the average person is prone to become distracted and detour from his intended path. In this excellent book Dr Bill Newman reveals those road blocks in the pursuit of success. To know your enemy is the first step in defeating him. Brilliant in its simplicity and wisdom, this book fulfils a great need in the average person who, in the pursuit of his dreams, seeks to become above average. I highly recommend this book. Well done, Bill Newman!

...John Hargreaves

CONTENTS

THIS BOOK CAN CHANGE YOUR LIFE!

Often when reading a book we decide to apply what we read to our lives. All too often, weeks later, we have forgotten our good intentions. Here are 5 practical ways of:-

TURNING GOOD INTENTIONS INTO PRACTICAL HABITS
1. USE CARDS
Write out the principles or passages you want to memorise on 3" x 5" cards and review them often.

2. MARK YOUR CALENDAR
Mark your calendar daily for the time when you will review your good intentions.

3. RE-READ YOUR UNDERLINES
Underline key portions of this book, then re-read your underlines over and over.

4. APPLY THE MATERIAL IMMEDIATELY
There is an old saying:

> Here something - you forget it,
> See something - you remember it, and
> Do something - you understand it.

Apply what you learn as soon as you possibly can - it helps you understand and remember it.

5. PRIORITISE WHAT YOU WANT TO LEARN

Select 1-3 things from the book, apply them faithfully and make them a habit. Remember, every person alive struggles with turning their good intentions into habits. Using these 5 points will turn wishing into doing.

INTRODUCTION

KEYS TO HELP YOU CONQUER THE TEN MOST COMMON CAUSES OF FAILURE

Very often we are our own worst enemy as we foolishly build stumbling blocks on the road that leads to success and happiness.

"Beware of no one more than yourself; we carry our own worst enemies within us."
[Charles Spurgeon]

You have this book because you want your life to count - to mean something. You know your life is filled with a sense of purpose, meaning and destiny.

It hurts me when I see those whose minds are closed. Our minds are like parachutes - they function only when open! No one knows less than the one who knows it all.

As my dear friend, Tom Avelsgaard, says, *"You need to feed the goose that lays the golden egg."*

Investing in your life does exactly that. That is the purpose of this book. Don't waste your life - you only have one life. Give it your best shot.

There are, I believe, ten basic causes of failure. If you know them you can conquer them. No one else can handle them for you. Others can help but, ultimately, it is up to you.

Everyone has tough times in life which can easily distract and detour us from real achievement in life. You may feel like Rocky where you have hit the canvas so many times but, like him, you've got to say, *"I ain't going down no more!"*

I read the following story in Max Lucado's brilliant book, "In the Eye of the Storm". You may relate well to it.

Chippie the parakeet never saw it coming - one second he was peacefully perched in his cage, the next he was sucked in, washed up and blown over!

The problems began when Chippie's owner decided to clean Chippie's cage with a vacuum cleaner. She removed the attachment from the end of the hose and stuck it in the cage. The phone rang, she turned to pick it up, she barely said "hello", when - "sssopp!" - Chippie got sucked in!

The bird owner gasped, put down the phone, turned off the vacuum and opened the back. There was Chippie - still alive, but stunned.

Since the bird was covered with dust and soot she grabbed him and raced to the bathroom, turned on the tap and held Chippie under the running water. Then, realising that Chippie was soaked and shivering she did what any compassionate bird owner would do ... she ran for the hairdryer and blasted the pet with hot air.

Poor Chippie never knew what hit him.

A few days after the trauma the reporter who had initially written about the event contacted Chippie's owner to see how the bird was recovering. "Well", she replied, "Chippie doesn't sing much anymore - he just sits and stares".

It is not hard to see why "sucked in, washed up and blown over" is enough to steal the song from the stoutest heart!

Can you relate to Chippie? Most of us can. One minute you are seated in familiar territory with a song on your lips, then ... the pink slip comes; the rejection letter arrives; the door closes; the divorce paper are delivered; the cheque bounces; the policeman knocks at the door.

"Sssopp!" You are sucked into a black cavern of doubts, doused with the cold water of reality and stung with the

hot air of empty promises.

The life that has been calm is now so stormy. You're hail-stormed by demands, assailed by doubts, pummelled by questions and, somewhere in the trauma, you lose your joy. Somewhere in the storm you lose your song.

You - like Chippie - may have hit a few storms in life which have blown you off track. You alone have the unique ability to choose whether you are going to just park there beside the road or turn on your indicator and say, *"I aim to get on the road again".*

Success is getting up one more time than you fall.

Whether you believe it or not your life is a Rolls Royce. It's time to roll out on to the highway, to put yourself in cruise control, to get somewhere in life. I know it is more comfortable and controlled staying in the car back in the garage, but you will never discover some distant city by just staying there.

It's time to hit -

"THE ROAD TO SUCCESS".

YOU ARE SPECIAL
There is only one
YOU

Think about that. Your face and features, your voice, your style, your background, your characteristics and peculiarities, your abilities, your smile, your walk your handshake, your manner of expression, your viewpoint ... everything about you is found in only one individual since mankind first began - YOU.

Dig as deeply as you please in the ancient, dusty archives of Homo Sapiens and you'll not find another YOU in the whole lot. That, by the way, did not "just happen"; it was planned that way. Why? Because God wanted you to be YOU, that's why.

You were designed to be a unique, distinct, significant person unlike any other individual on the face of the earth, throughout the vast expanse of time. In your case, as in the case of every other human being, the mould was broken, never to be used again, once you entered the flow of mankind.

YOU HAD BETTER BELIEVE IT ...
YOU ARE SPECIAL

BLAMING OTHERS

This is one of the classic detours on the road to success. *"No wonder I can't get along this highway any better. Others are passing me. It must be the way those turkeys put this car together!!"*

We are masters at pinning the blame on others when things aren't going our way. The schoolboy blames the teacher, the motorist blames the other drivers. The husband shouts at his wife. The employee laments, *"The company doesn't appreciate me."*

Then there's the government! It amazes me that, even in some countries when the government is appalling, yet those in business with a will to win will still be successful despite which party is in power. You see the real battle is not with the others but with ourselves.

Obstacles are what you see when you take your eye off the goals!

It is a tough road to the top but the view is well worth it. There has never been a truly successful person who has just had it all handed to him or her. The easiest "cop out" is to blame others instead of looking into the mirror and saying, *"The buck stops here. I am personally responsible for my own success or failure."*

What is it that bugs you, that stops your progress? You know - frogs have it easy, they can eat what bugs them! Perhaps you need to analyse what is bugging you. Why aren't you in top gear instead of still crawling along in first. First gear makes a lot of noise and sounds like there's plenty of grunt but you can't stay there the whole of your life, otherwise you will get nowhere.

"But you don't understand all my problems. I feel like I'm snowed under. The bills keep piling in."

Listen - birds have bills too, but they keep on singing!

Turn your problems into a propeller. The only place in town where people have no problems is out at the local cemetery! Wrapped up in each problem and hardship is a golden opportunity. There is a lesson to learn, an opportunity to seize. Learn to be lateral in your thinking. Snap out of seeing the problems, instead see the potential.

It has been well said, *"Until you believe in yourself you won't believe in your future"*.

If you keep on telling yourself that the reason you have to crawl down the road of life is because of the tough deals you have received from others, you will never get anywhere. We beat ourselves before we even start by telling ourselves we cannot do it. I heard of a man telling of his golf experiences. When he was about to take a shot his friend said, *"Be careful, don't put it in the water."*

He said, *"I couldn't have put it more perfectly in the water if I had tried."* In his next shot he centred his mind on hitting the ball to the green. You guessed it - it landed on the green. Our actions follow our minds. It is so important to realise the influence you have on yourself as you speak to your mind. We need to be very careful what we say to ourselves!

You may have reason to complain but you must choose to smile.

As I have observed the immigrants who have come to our country, they are four times more likely to become wealthy because they arrive with an attitude of hope, excitement and gratitude.

Instead of the pity parties we need to start cracking the whip on ourselves. If we want it better tomorrow we must start today - NOW. It takes commitment and discipline. Discipline is the refining fire by which talent becomes ability. I seriously doubt that there has ever been an undisciplined person who was a champion regardless of their field of endeavour.

You must be decisive and take action. *"If you've got to swallow a frog you don't want to look at that sucker too long!"*

Stop blaming others. Be decisive. Start now. Take charge of your life. Be a thermometer not a thermostat - one monitors the temperature, the other controls it.

It's not what happens to you but how you handle what happens to you that makes the difference.

Dr J Allan Peterson, in his monthly publication "Better Families", said it well:

"Everyone at one time or another has felt like a complete failure. Many have allowed the fear of failure to destroy them. Actually fear is far more destructive than failure and, in any area of life, fear of failure can defeat you before you get started."

Always remember - failure is an event, never a person; an attitude, not an outcome. It is a stepping stone teaching you something and adding to your experience.

Stop blaming others for your situation. The heaviest thing

to carry is a grudge. Forgive and forget. We need to stop lashing out with our tongues. Having a sharp tongue can cut your own throat!

"Forgiveness is the key that unlocks the door of resentment and the handcuffs of hate. It is a power that breaks the chains of bitterness and the shackles of selfishness".
[William Arthur Ward]

The one who cannot forgive destroys the bridge over which he himself must pass.

It is time to scrap the "born-to-lose" syndrome. There is a Chinese proverb which says that all you have to do to beat a man down is to tell him ten times a day that he is worthless. You, or someone else, has been telling yourself that for too long and it is a lie. You are special and you CAN do it.

Friend - it's time to change gears. Get out of low, you're chewing up too much petrol anyway. Get moving. You may still be chugging along on the service road while thousands are cruising down the highway.

Take a look - the light is green -

GO!

Chapter
2

BLAMING YOURSELF

Here is the second of our detours. This detour can prove to be a disaster for you unless you lick it. This person is driving along while others are passing. They say to themselves, *"Why didn't I have a better vehicle? Look at what the others are driving. I wish I had that BMW or that Merc., or that Rolls. Look at my beat up old jalopy. Why couldn't I have a better model?"*

"Why do I always say the wrong thing?" *"Why do I always put my foot in it?"* So many become insecure with feelings of inferiority.

"My great concern is not whether you have failed but whether you are content with your failure."
[Abraham Lincoln]

This is what Zig Zigler calls the P.L.O.M. disease (poor little ol' me). I hope you are not inflicted with it. It is rampant today.

This is one lane that you must not travel in - it is going to "Nowheresville".

You may have physical problems or have had a tough start in life. It is time to stop the pity-party.

It's not where you come from - it's where you are going that counts. Where you come from is not as important as where you are going.

Seventy-five percent of the three hundred, world-class leaders in a recent study were raised in proverty, had been abused as children, or had some serious physical disability.

Where you start doesn't matter and what your parents or ancestors did is not the determining factor in what you do.

Quit blaming your poor education. When you don't have an education you've got to use your brains! Stop blaming the "mess ups" of yesterday. Don't let yesterday use up today.

Start getting tough on yourself. If you want a place in the sun be prepared to put up with a few blisters! It's still true - a turtle only makes progress when it sticks its neck out. If you must cry over spilt milk please try and condense it! Life requires effort. You don't have to brush all your teeth - only the ones you want to keep!

It's time to get out of the slow lane that you are travelling in.

When Major General William F Dean was released by his communist captors a newsman asked what sustained him during his three years of misery. *"I never felt sorry for myself,"* the general replied, *"and that's what licked it."*

Always remember - past failures are guideposts for future success.

"Failure is, in a sense, the highway to success inasmuch as every discovery of what is false leads us to seek earnestly after what is true."
- John Keats

Mistakes mark the road to success. He who makes no mistakes makes no progress. Make sure you generate a reasonable number of mistakes. I know that comes naturally to some people but too many people are so afraid of error that they make their lives rigid with checks and counterchecks, discourage change and, in the end, so structure themselves that they will miss the kind of offbeat opportunity that can send their life skyrocketing.

So take a look at your record and, if you come to the end of a year and see that you haven't made many mistakes, ask yourself if you have tried everything you should have.

It is a cliche to say that we learn by our mistakes so I'll state the case more strongly than that. I'll say that you can't learn without mistakes. One reason some people never grow through change is that they can't stand failure. Even the best people have a lot more failure than success. The secret is that they don't let the failures upset them. They do their very best. Let the chips fall where they may, then go on the the next attempt.

I remember once driving off the highway to a rest area some years ago. There had been a fresh fall of heavy rain previously. I drove to what I thought was a nice grassy spot only to sink in mud to my axles. My car wheels were spinning but I was going nowhere. Even a truck could not pull me out. Then a tow truck just happened to be passing by! Without his help I would have been stuck there for the night.

The "poor little ol' me" syndrome will get us stuck in the mud every time. Watch the "pity parties". Stop sitting in a heap staring at your navel, saying, *"I can't do it."* You can do it. Your partner is depending on you, your family is depending on you, your true friends are depending on you. There are those who are looking to your leadership. If you go negative it will be like a plague that will sweep right through your family, work and social situation.

Self pity is just pure selfishness. Selfishness turns life into a burden. Unselfishness turns burdens into life!

Everyone has been wounded at some time or another. We may disguise our wounds behind a smile and keep our guard up. But if we really searched our lives we would find that every person has a secret pain, an intimate agony, a private hurt with wounds deep inside.

Society inflicts wounds on us. Some may have been the victim of racial or ethnic prejudice or some other form of discrimination such as sexism or "age-ism". Perhaps you have been laughed at or, worse still, ignored.

Sometimes those who are closest to you inflict the deepest wounds. Perhaps it was the hurtful memory of what a father or mother, a spouse, child, lover, employer, teacher or friend did to you.

Your past cannot be changed but you can change tomorrow by your actions today.

There is nothing that has ever happened to you or anyone else that cannot be forgiven.

There are other hidden wounds we inflict on ourselves. Perhaps you react too negatively to circumstances or maybe you take yourself too seriously. We may read too much into other people's actions and exaggerate their rejection of us.

If you want to be distressed - look within.
If you want to be defeated   - look back.
If you want to be distracted - look around.
If you want to be dismayed - look ahead.
If you want to be delivered   - look up!

Everyone who has ever lived has experienced hurt in one form or another by words, looks, actions.

How do you handle the hurts and bitterness in your life? I have said many times:

Don't <u>nurse</u> your hurts
Don't <u>curse</u> your hurts (causing you bitterness)
Don't <u>rehearse</u> your hurts

But you must <u>immerse</u> them. Bury them in service to others.

You must <u>reverse</u> them. Turn the whole thing around so that you may become a more sensitive, compassionate, caring, thoughtful and gracious person.

Whatever you give away will always come back to you.

* Give a smile, not a scowl.
* Give a compliment, not a complaint.
* Give encouragement, not criticism.
* Give kind words, not cutting words.

Whatever you give away will always come back to you - positive or negative. Give a little, you get a little back. Give a lot, you get a lot back.

The sooner you realise that life is not fair, the sooner you will reach emotional maturity.

REMEMBER : Some people are like teabags - not much good until they go through some hot water!!

Don't look at what others have. Use what you have. Get out of the mud and get back onto the highway. Change gears. Get out of that slow lane. Get your eyes off your problems. Start seeing your potential.

He who chooses the beginning of a road also chooses its outcome.

HAVING NO GOALS

This is the person who turns off the highway too soon. They then head out to a little, but very crowded, place called "Someday Isle". You know - *"Someday I'll do this"* or *"Someday I'll do that"* or *"Someday I'll go here or there"*. *"Someday I'll get started."* *Someday I will begin to build a business"*. *"Someday I'll begin to do something with my life - someday"*.

They wait for something to turn up; meanwhile they turn everything down. It's beneath them, beyond them, or not what they are suited for, or perhaps they just don't like it. They wait for the Fairy Prince/Princess on the Dream Boat to come along.

According to Richard L Evans of the Detroit Times, it isn't always clear - perhaps it's seldom clear - just what we are waiting for, but some of us persist in waiting so chronically that youth slips by, opportunities slip by and life slips by, finding us still waiting for something that has been going on all the time... But when in the world are we going to begin to live as though we understand the urgency of life? This is our time, our day, our generation...not some golden age of the past, not some Utopia of the future...this is it...whether we are thrilled or disappointed, busy or bored. This is life...and it is passing...what are we waiting for?

Almost no one applauds an entrepreneur until they succeed. Therefore they must look inward for support. The essential ingredients for entrepreneurship are a vision, a sense of mission and a will to keep going forward when everyone else is telling you to go back.

It won't be brains, brawn, skill or a business plan (as good as all these are) that will result in your ultimate success. It will be persistence, pure and simple.

Always remember Walt Disney and Mickey Mouse didn't quit and didn't succeed until the 303rd bank. Finally Disney found a banker who believed in him and his idea enough to get him started.

You may find that, in the incubation stage of a venture, it may be better to keep your dreams to yourself and keep your own counsel until your idea becomes strong enough to withstand the inevitable criticism from outside forces.

But hold tight to your vision. Nearly everyone with whom you share your dream will attempt to alter it, if only slightly, with his or her own input. Be clear in your own mind what you want to accomplish.

Avoid distraction at all costs.

It is true that tough times come for everyone, but it is also true that the source of most tough times is lack of direction. Once you have a single goal that you can visibly see you will be unstoppable. Remember - a 100% commitment to one goal is more than twice as good as a 50% commitment to two goals. The difference between doing and dabbling is focus.

It may not be fair but it is a fact that it is not good enough to be "just as good" as everyone else out there. You have to be better.

Strive to be as good as you can possibly be in presenting your product, plan or performance. It is what an athlete calls their P.B. - their personal best.

It would be totally foolish to drive out on the highway without knowing where you are heading. It is just as foolish to embark on this precious span of time we call life without knowing what we want to do with it.

If you don't know exactly where you are going then how can you prepare? Do you have enough fuel, do the tyres have enough tread? What about the battery? When was the motor serviced last? Preparation and planning are needed.

So it is with your life and mine. It is amazing how many have no plans or goals for their life and will sit and criticise anyone who has.

Take the goals off the basketball court or the football field and you will have chaos; have fairways but no greens with holes on the golf course and you will be doing what so many in life are doing - running round in circles.

No - if at the moment you recognise you have taken a detour by turning off the highway too soon, take a look at the sign coming up - "U-TURNS PERMITTED"! If you are going in the wrong direction, going nowhere or to "Someday Isle", then right now determine that you will do a radical U-turn.

To help you in establishing some priorities and to set some real goals for your life, I would like to quote from my book, "Soaring with Eagles".

GOALSETTING AND THE ACHIEVER

Goals are vision with feet. Goals are a set of specific, measurable steps to achieve the vision. When realistic goals are set and met, you will feel satisfied and successful. The whole concept of setting goals will have the exciting flavour of accomplishment. Goalsetting will deliver you from crisis management. You switch from fire fighting to fire prevention.

Goalsetting will help you to constantly resharpen your vision. An axeman never loses time sharpening his axe. Take time to hone and rehone your goals.

Here are some of the benefits of goalsetting:

1. Goals simplify the decision-making process.
   The achiever is constantly faced with a multitude of decisions. Invitations to join this Board or that, to speak at conventions and meetings, a thousand and one opportunities come. His/her gift makes way for them. Others feel they can organise your life better than you can. When you know your direction in life as you establish goals, so you can evaluate simply and easily each situation as it presents itself.

2. Goals tone up mental and physical health.
   The reason so many people die soon after retirement is that they have ceased to set goals for themselves. Without direction in your life you are vulnerable to negative thought patterns. It is well known that your mental attitude and your physical health are closely related. Having set goals will demand that you keep sharp, mentally and physically in shape.

3. <u>Goals generate respect.</u>

4. <u>Goals help you to realise and enjoy the feeling of accomplishment.</u> What you cannot measure you cannot monitor. Without goals you float aimlessly, but as you achieve your goals there is a feeling of satisfaction and accomplishment.

5. <u>Goals produce persistence.</u>
   Persistence, or staying power, is the quality that sets the leader apart. Just as the stamp sticks to the letter until it gets there, so the achiever never gives up.

   Eagles are remarkably patient birds, a quality that seems almost obsolete in this day of instant coffee, instant food, instant delivery - instant everything. Yet this bird, with its mastery of flight, its deadly beak and razor sharp talons, its extra keen eyesight and legendary boldness has great need for this quality of patience.

   During hunting, often the eagle will miss its prey and would otherwise go hungry but for its ability to quietly and patiently wait it out. Eagles have been observed roosting for hours above a rabbit hole, snake hole or place where a fish or bird had disappeared. The raptor will wait and wait, sometimes for hours on end. Usually the bird's patience is rewarded and the prey will show its head and, like lightning, the eagle strikes with devastating speed and power.
   Problems and discouragements will face the achiever,

but he can overcome them with staying power.

Many times we are nearer our goals than we think we are, so never give up - persist. It's always too soon to quit.

6. <u>Goals deliver the achiever from the deception and desire to applause.</u>
   Achievers become unstuck when they start to believe their own publicity! It is always a fact of life that a third of the crowd care for you, a third of the crowd don't care for you and the other third couldn't care less about you! That should bring you down to earth.

7. <u>Goals deliver you from living in the past.</u>
   An achiever, often because of his hard work, will receive justified praise. The problem arises when his ego needs to feed on it.

Having set goals the leader takes his mind off the past and centres his attention on the future.

Your most powerful weapon against limiting thoughts is your willingness to clarify and envision what you truly want.

The advantages of goalsetting

The establishment of a goals' programme is the way you can fulfil your vision. Setting goals is not a one-time exercise. It is an ongoing discipline. Without a goals' programme a vision is only wishful thinking. Your goals will have to be constantly modified. While you are working on your immediate, or short-range goals, you must be careful to keep your eyes on your long-range goals.

Your vision must remain permanent but your goals must remain flexible. Do not change the order. Far too many allow their vision to change and make their goals permanent.

It is time now to practically and systematically set out your goals. Remember, goals are a set of specific, measurable steps that design the programme for fulfilling your vision.

1. Make a list of your goals.
   Write down all the goals that you can think of in the four areas - being - doing - owning - accomplishing. Start with 20 years then 15, then 10, then 5, then 1 year, then 6 months, then 90 days, then 60 days.

2. Now rearrange them in order of priority for each of the four areas. Select the goals you want first. Next set a target date. Be realistic. Make them attainable goals. A goal without a deadline is not really a goal...it is a wish.

3. Make a list of the required action you must take to achieve your goal. For example the extra effort

required, or more study, or the cash needed. (Remember - no gain without pain)

4. Develop the qualities in your personal behaviour that will be required. Obtain the skills. For example - a pleasant personality, neat appearance, mental awareness, a winning smile, a warm handshake, a positive walk or plain hard work.

5. List your deficiencies and conquer them, starting right now! Today!

6. List the personnel or help needed to achieve your goals and the techniques or methods as well.

7. Develop an iron will determination to follow through your plans regardless of obstacles, criticism or circumstances, or what other people say, think or do.

8. Visualise the new you. Vividly imagine yourself as having already reached your goals.

9. Begin at once.

In the absence of clearly defined goals we are forced to concentrate on activity and ultimately become enslaved by it. Remember, there is no joy in victory without running the risk of defeat.

<u>Opportunities never come to those who wait - they are captured by those who dare to attack.</u>

The fulfilment of our goals must be good for others. If they bring harm to others, then our goals are selfish. The great rewards in life are love and achievement. All else is secondary. Become a giver - not a getter.

Don't be afraid to set goals.

To achieve goals demands hard work, determination and commitment. For many, though, the main reason they do not establish a quest to achieve goals is plain fear; the fear of ridicule from others or the fear of defeat. Others fear their goals will not be perfect - or worse still, they may consider themselves presumptuous.

The importance and the benefit of goalsetting is immeasurable. Without setting goals your visions and dreams are just wishful thinking. There are so many benefits in goalsetting. They make decision making easier. Your physical and mental health are better. You have established a positive attitude to life. You are helping to eliminate stress, confusion and fear. Those who have goals attract respect from people. It gives you a sense of accomplishment. It gives you "stickability" and staying power. It is staying power that sets the leader apart.

The tragedy of life doesn't lie in not reaching your goal; the tragedy lies in having no goal to reach.

Henry Kaiser said, "Determine what you want more than anything else in life, write down the means by which you intend to attain it and permit nothing to deter you from pursuing it."

Without goals and priorities we will never escape the tyranny of the urgent. If we do not have our eyes fixed on a goal the urgent will crowd out the important.

The only difference between being a "dreamer" and a "goalsetter" is adding a deadline to the dream.

Goalsetting accomplishes your vision.

Don't be satisfied with average performance. Set some real goals and go after them.

Don't turn off this highway too soon. "Someday Isle" is very attractive but, in stopping there, you will never reach your dreams and the true fulfillment and potential of your life.

If you are looking in the right direction then you won't take the wrong turn.

CHOOSING THE WRONG GOALS

Here is the fourth detour that we have to avoid while we are travelling down the road to success.

Make sure that you don't follow the wrong signs. Just as there are many signs as we drive down the highway enticing us to go here or to go there, so in life there are so many voices calling out to us to do this or to do that. We must determine within ourselves what are the goals that we want in life? What do we want to achieve? Where do we want to go?

It would be a great sadness to discover, after many years of struggle, that attaining the object of your efforts did not bring happiness. No one wants to climb the ladder of success only to discover that the ladder was leaning against the wrong wall!

Success is a series of right choices. Each day we stand at a fork in the road. When we say "yes" to one activity we must say "no" to another. The key is not to zig-zag through life. I would sooner be a pile driver than a confetti sprinkler any day! If you follow all the signs and chase all the goals you will get nowhere in life.

The Aboriginal people of Australia, on their walkabouts years ago, had a method of getting to their destinations as quickly as possible. If they were to cross a vast expanse of land they would set a goal away on the horizon. It may have been a tree or even a mountain. During the journey (which may have taken hours or even days) every time they rested, stopped to eat or drink they would again reset their goal and move towards that goal. In this way they would not wander about, they would get to their destination as quickly as possible.

It is the same way in our journey through life. Unless we have got our eyes fixed clearly on the goals that we want to achieve in life, we will zig-zag through life and not achieve as much as we wished to.

The first thing you must do is to clearly define in your own mind what your visions and goals are - what are the things that you want to achieve in your life? Ask yourself - where am I now and where do I ultimately want to go? If you want to be an achiever you must start putting your life together. Ask yourself - what kind of person do I really want to be? How would I carry myself to become that kind of person? What sort of clothes would I wear? How would I act? What would my speech be like? How would I relate to others?

If you know where you are going you won't be tempted to follow the wrong signs every time they turn up as you are travelling down the highway of life.

It is so much easier for shoppers going into a supermarket to make up a list prior to going. In this way they will not be running around all over the store looking at every item and all over the shelves. Rather they will go to where they need to go and choose exactly what they want to have.

Make sure that you have a road map to follow. Road maps provide the information that you need in order to get to your destination. In the same way map out the course that you want to take in life. Determine the destination that you want to seek to achieve and then choose the right vehicle that you want to get into to get there. You may be frantically busy but it is crucial that you sit down and start dreaming some dreams and determining where you want to go in life and what you want to achieve with your life.

You have been presented with an invaluable treasure, the treasure of a life. Don't squander it, don't waste it. Make it effective. Make your life exciting. Make it a challenge, make it an adventure.

Give yourself some high and lofty goals, things that you really want to achieve in life. Seize with both hands the challenges and the opportunities of life.

The story is told about the time Napoleon's steed got away from him. An alert private jumped on his own horse and chased down the general's horse. When he presented the reins of the animal to Napoleon the ruler took them, smiled at his willing private and said, *"Thank you, Captain."* The soldier's eyes widened at what he had heard. He straightened, saluted and snapped, *"Thank you, sir"*.

He immediately went to the barracks, collected his bags, moved into the officers' quarters, took his old uniform to the quartermaster and exchanged it for that of a captain. By the general's word he had become a private-turned-commissioned-officer. He didn't argue, didn't shrug, he didn't doubt. He knew that the one who had the power to do it had done it and he accepted that.

If you are on the lookout, opportunities are going to come your way. Be alert for them, make sure that you are heading in the right direction and don't follow the wrong signs. Make sure that you don't end up at the wrong destination.

A pastor was leaving his pastorate and some friends sent him flowers as a going-away gesture. But the florist got the flowers meant for the pastor mixed up with flowers that were supposed to go to a funeral. The next day the pastor was laughing with the florist. The pastor remarked, *"I was wondering why there was a sympathy card in my flowers."* The florist said, *"I am not really worried about that, but the flowers that I sent to the funeral with your card in it read 'Best of luck in your new location'!"*

If you choose the wrong goals and follow the wrong signs in life you, too, may very well end up in the wrong location. People may be sincere in what they are doing with their lives, but you know you can be sincerely wrong.

I heard about a football player who was knocked on the head as he was playing in opposition to the other team. He saw the ball lying on the ground. I guess he was a little hazy and dizzy after the blow that he had received. He grabbed the ball quickly and started running down the field. The crowd was screaming at him, *"Stop! Stop! Stop!"* But he couldn't hear them and he didn't listen. All that he could see was the goal post ahead. He put the ball over the try line, only to discover that he had scored a goal for the opposing team by putting the ball over his own try line!

People may be sincere in life but they can be heading in the wrong direction. Make sure you are not one of them.

Someone is reported to have asked a concert violinist in New York's Carnegie Hall how she became so skilled. She said that it was by "<u>planned neglect</u>". She planned to neglect everything that was not related to her goal.

Someone asked Isaac Newton, *"How did you discover the law of gravity?"* His reply - *"By thinking about it all the time"*. Make sure that you are thinking about your destination in life all the time. Keep your mind on where you are going.

It was the great Emerson who said, *"Beware of what you set your mind on for that you will surely become"*.

Victor Hugo said it well - *"There is nothing so powerful in this world as an idea whose time has come"*.

One day a young man had an accident. He was struck with a thought! Oliver Wendell Holmes said, *"Man's mind, stretched to a new idea, never goes back to its original dimensions."*

It is still true - small minds discuss persons, average minds discuss events, great minds discuss ideas.

Psychologists say that 10,000 thoughts go through a human mind in one day, that is 3 million, 500 thousand per year. That is a good reason for bringing our thoughts under control. No wonder we are so apt to go off on different tracks instead of keeping our minds on our goals.

Here are a set of affirmations which you may like to use every day to keep you on track:

Today is my day

Today my thoughts are centred on expecting only the best and giving only the best.

Today my mind and heart are open to new opportunties and I make the most out of every situation.

Today I will smile and act enthusiastically in everything I do. I will make every person I meet feel very important and I will show them that I care.

Today I will develop strong, healthy relationships with those around me and I will only ever look for the good in those people. I like people and people like me.

Today my confidence is high and I am willing to step out and take a chance.
I speak freely to all those I meet.
I know I have something valuable to contribute.
I expect results today and my time is well invested.

Today I am one step closer to achieving my goals and dreams. I always keep my eyes focused on success and achievement.

Today I will sow good seed so that I reap my harvest of reward.

Today is my day

To keep yourself on track and on the right road let me encourage you now to practically and systematically set out your goals. Remember - goals are a set of specific measurable steps that design the programme for fulfilling your vision.

Don't be afraid to set goals. The importance and benefit of goal-setting is immeasurable. Without setting goals your visions and dreams are just wishful thinking. There are so many benefits in goal-setting. They make decision making easier. Your physical and mental health are better. You have established a positive attitude to life. You are helping to eliminate stress, confusion and fear. Those who have goals attract respect from people. It gives you a sense of accomplishment. It gives you "stickability" and staying power.

The FBI went into a town to investigate the work of, what appeared to be, a sharpshooter. They were amazed to find many bullseyes drawn around town with bullets that had penetrated the exact centre of the targets. When they finally found the man who had been doing the shooting they asked him about the technique he used to obtain such accuracy. The answer was simple - he shot the bullet first then drew the bullseye later!

So it is with the goals that we make in life - we should use them to direct our work and determine if we have accomplished our purposes not to defend what we happen to do.

The Californian coast was shrouded in fog on the morning of 4 July 1952. 21 miles to the west on Catalina Island a 34 year old woman waded into the water and began swimming towards California, determined to be the first woman ever to swim the 21 mile strait. Her name was Florence Chadwick and she had already been the first woman to swim the English Channel in both directions.

The water was numbing cold that morning and the fog was so thick that Chadwick could hardly see the boats in her own party - there to scare away the sharks. As the hours ticked by she swam on. Fatigue had never been a serious problem, there was only the bone-chilling cold of the water that was threatening.

More than 15 hours later, numb with the cold, the swimmer asked to be taken out. She could not go on any longer. Her mother and her trainer, in a boat alongside her, urged Chadwick to go on as they were getting close to shore. Yet all that she could see was dense fog. A few minutes later the swimmer was taken out of the water and later, realising that she had been within half a mile of the shore, she blurted out, *"I'm not excusing myself but if I could only have seen the shore I might have made it."*

Florence Chadwick had been licked, not by the cold or even the fatigue, but by the fog. The fog had obscured her goal, had blinded her reason and her eyes.

Don't let your life get fogged up. Spend some time, get some clear visions of where you want to go in life. Set good goals, the right goals for you and don't swerve off and choose the wrong goals and follow the wrong signs.

Chapter

5

THE SHORT CUT

> **There is no short cut to life.**
> **To the end of our days**
> **life is a lesson imperfectly learned.**
> - Harrison E Salisbury

Now we come to the fifth detour that you must avoid on your road to success.

This is the short cut. This is the road that, seemingly, would lead to "Easy City". Can you see the bright, blinking lights saying - "To Easy City" coming up before you? This is the person who doesn't like to get out of their comfort zone. They want to get to their destination the easiest way they possibly can, with no struggle in life.

An electric current will follow the line of least resistance but a light bulb glows precisely because there is resistance. Be careful in life - if the going is getting easy it may be because you are going downhill! Few people travel the road to success without a puncture or two. Always remember a smooth sea never made a skilled sailor. There can be no rainbow without a cloud and a storm. Bob Hope, the comedian, was asked one time why he did not retire and go fishing. His reply was classic - *"The fish don't applaud!"*

Triumph is just "umph" added to "try". Hard work is the yeast that raises the dough! It is still true that the only place where success comes before work is in the dictionary! Ideas won't work unless YOU do! We must work hard because the future is purchased by the present. The hard work we do today will ensure success in our future.

"There is no labour a man can't do that's undignified - if he does it right." - Bill Cosby

I read, a while ago, about a man who had not received a promotion he thought he deserved. Not only that, a younger man had been given the promotion. So this disgruntled employee went to his boss and complained. *"I can't see how you can give that man the job. After all I have been here faithfully serving the company for years. I have twenty years' experience."*

Without blinking an eye his boss looked straight at him and replied, *"No, you haven't had twenty years' experience - you have had one year's experience and have repeated it twenty times."*

Beware in life of the alluring signs that call us to drive out to "Easy City".

During the American Revolution a man in civilian clothes rode past a group of soldiers repairing a small defensive barrier. The leader was shouting instructions at them, but making no attempt to help them. Asked why by the rider, the leader said with great dignity, *"Sir, I am a corporal"*. The stranger apologised, dismounted and proceeded to help the exhausted soldiers. The job done, he turned to corporal and said, *"If you need some more help, son, call me."* With that the Commander-in-Chief, George Washington, rode away. Little wonder he became such a great leader. He was a man who was prepared to get his hands dirty.

Don't fear the struggles in life. Very often they are the things that develop our character. The very issues and circumstances that first appear as road blocks to our success can often be used as levers that make success a reality. The key is to attack these road blocks and setbacks with creativity. Creativity simply means the ability to understand your environment or conditions and use your environment or conditions to your advantage.

We must stop dissipating our energy and becoming obsessed with our problems by fighting against the situation.

Far too many people in problem situations act like total non-swimmers. If you put a non-swimmer in a boat, take him out about a mile from shore and toss him into the water, what will he do? Certainly he will try to swim, but, in his panic, he will fight the water. The more he thrashes about - the more he fights the water - the sooner his energy is dissipated and he drowns.

Place a professional swimmer in the same situation. He will do something quite different. First he will relax and float or tread water. In treading water the expert swimmer uses the environment and conditions to sustain himself. Next he will select a shoreline destination. Then, at a reasonable pace, keeping the shoreline objective in sight all the while, he will swim to shore. Throughout the entire sequence of events he uses the water, his environment, as the means to the desired result. Whenever we abandon our objective we begin to drown because we have lost our creativity.

Our educational system has conditioned us to view as a threat any situation that may disrupt our plans. For the most part, while in school we are taught that we must have "the right answer" which conditions us to have a one-answer mentality. That may be true in mathematics. However in the business world things are far more viable. "There is always more than one way to skin a cat."

When you are in a tough situation, ask yourself the question, *"How? How can I use this situation or condition to my advantage?"* The key is to know what your goals are. But then use lateral thinking in order to achieve those goals.

The buzz word today is fractals. It is going to change our whole way of thinking. Most of the patterns in nature (clouds, trees, waves, etc.) are fractal forms, that is never-repeating, common-shaped structures. In creation things have both same-ness and difference. Snowflakes are all the same and yet no two are the same. They all have a different pattern. Clouds are the same way. Plant, leaves - all the same, yet no two the same. In some way they are all different. With all the millions of people born there have been no two exactly alike.

We are moving in a constantly changing creation. Take your body for instance. Your skin is new every month, your liver every six weeks, your brain about every 12 months. In spite of all this change we remain rather constant due to the organising function of information in our DNA.

What is a cell? It is memory that has built matter around itself forming a specific pattern. Your body is just the place that your memory cells call home.

People would like to structure their lives, to know that everything is under tight control, but in actual fact that is not real life. I am sorry but I have news for you - life is not just going to be comfortable for you. The so-called short cut to "Easy City" will lead you to the destination of something which is just as hard anyway.

In real life the issue is not control but dynamic connectedness. The whole universe and our world is in constant motion and change. Life is constantly moving and we must learn to adapt and move with it. I am sorry to tell you but the comfort zone is just an illusion. What is desperately needed in our life is a will to win and an ability to compete.

The great football coach, Vince Lombardi, said it well: *"In truth I have never known a man worth his salt who, in the long run, deep within his heart, did not appreciate the grind, the discipline. There is something in good men that really yearns for, and needs, discipline and the harsh reality of head-to-head combat."*

He also said, *"Winning is not a some-time thing, it is an all-the-time thing. You don't win once in a while, you don't do things right once in a while, you do them right all the time. Winning is a habit. Unfortunately so is losing."*

Life is tough and we are all going to make mistakes. I don't think I have ever made a <u>small</u> mistake in my life. But that's where you will find success - on the other side of failure.

As a boy riding horses I learnt well that it is not how many times you fall off a horse but how many times you get back on. We have all made mistakes and we have all got our messes to clean up but winners in life focus on the present and the future, nôt on the past.

Hard work works and winners work hard. There is simply no substitute for putting in the hours. The best formula is - work smarter, faster and harder and remember, it is always better to work 100 hours for yourself than 40 hours for someone else. Act decisively with your life. Don't wait for your opportunities to come along. If you put off everything until you are sure of it you will get nothing done. We have to get serious and real about life.

I heard about a father who complained about the amount of time his family spent in front of the television. His children watched cartoons and neglected their school work. His wife preferred soap operas to housework. His solution *"as soon as the football season is over I am going to pull the plug!"*

Theodore Roosevelt said one time, *"There has never been a man in our history who has led a life of ease, whose name is worth remembering."*

No doubt you have heard about the conversation that is said to have taken place between a hen and a pig. When they passed a church and observed the subject of the pastor's sermon "How can we help the poor?", after a moment's reflection the hen said, *"I know how we can do it - we can give them a ham and egg breakfast."* The pig protested, saying, *"That breakfast would only be a contribution for you but for me it would mean total commitment."*

If we are to achieve anything in life it won't be because we are going to take the short cut to "Easy City" but it is going to take total commitment to our goals and desires and what we want to achieve.

Have you heard about the bank that had been robbed for the third time by the same bandit. A police inspector asked the teller, *"Did you notice anything special about the man?"* *"Yes,"* he said, *"he seemed better dressed each time."*

Keep at it. Don't let adversity keep you down. Every adversity you conquer will help you to get better at it. Every day, as you drive down the highway, you will see one sign after another saying "To Easy City". You must constantly make the choice whether you are going to go into a comfort zone or whether you are going to fight on to achieve your goals and dreams in life.

Taking the short cut may lead you into a dead end street.

Chapter

6

TAKING THE LONG ROAD

Can you imagine yourself driving down the highway, then you see this sign which says, "Tourist Route". Of course you will realise that this is a very scenic area but it is often the long way around. You know that it may take extra time to get back on the highway further down the road, but you are prepared to take the detour because you want to see the wonderful scenery.

With all my heart I believe that it is important in life to pause to enjoy the scenery, to smell the daisies, to enjoy the view while you are climbing that mountain. But what I am getting at here is the importance of not wasting time while we are going to our goals in life. Your time is the most precious thing that you have. Don't waste it and don't squander it.

One thing you cannot recycle is wasted time. Lost time is never found again. Taking the tourist route, the long way around, can often lead us in circles. We were never intended to act as does the pine caterpillar. Place a series of pine caterpillars end to end in a circle until the circle is closed and each will follow the caterpillar in front of it around the circle indefinitely. Place food at the centre of the circle and the caterpillars will continue to follow each other around that food until they die from starvation. The pine caterpillar is an instinct without imagination. It lacks the ability to seek any form of independent success on its own. It blindly adheres to a herd instinct, often to its detriment and even to its death.

To succeed means that you may have to step out of line and march to the sound of your own drummer.

The eminent psychologist, Dr Abraham Maslow, wrote: *"One can choose to go back towards safety or forward towards growth. Growth must be chosen again and again. Fear must be overcome again and again."*

So it is either forwards or backwards. That is the choice that is continually before us. We can either retreat and take the long way around - the tourist route - or we can choose to move forward to success.

You are totally responsible for the results that you obtain in life. It is you, it's not your mother, it's not your father, it's not your boss, it's not the brakes that control your life - it's you. Don't ever say, *"That's the way the ball bounces. That's the way the cookie crumbles, that's the way the mop flops."* You see, you must bounce your own ball. You have to crumble your own cookies, you have to flop your own mop! It is totally up to you.

Don't waste that life, you only have one shot at life. Don't waste that life, it is far too precious. If you were brought to the court and a charge was laid against you, that of a wasted life, how would you plead - guilty or not guilty? We must resist the tendency to believe that the world will come to us, that things will happen to us. No. We must go to it. This world will never meet you halfway.

There is nothing as sad as the people who spend their lives waiting for their ship to come in when they never send one out. Don't spend your life waiting for the big break. Your talent may be enormous, your potential may be great but talent and potential, unless effectively used, are wasted.

It is always easier to act tomorrow. The world is filled with "tomorrow people", those who will tell us, in no uncertain terms, that they are going to get started tomorrow - and tomorrow - and tomorrow ...

The fact is that no matter what we do, where we do it or when we start, we will never do it perfectly. There will never be just that right combination of circumstances that will make each and every major undertaking in our lives come off without a hitch. All that we can ever do is our best. I would rather try to succeed and fail than try to do nothing and succeed.

I know the way ahead may seem tough and the tourist route - the long way around - may seem irresistible. The situation that you are in at the moment may seem hard and you want to bail out.

Have you heard the story of the cranky grandpa who lay down to take a nap. To have a little fun his grandson put some limburger cheese on his moustache, Grandpa awoke with a snort and charged out of the bedroom saying, *"This room stinks!"* And through the house he went. He was finally forced outside only to find out that the whole world stank!

Sure the way ahead may be tough and hard but it is the way to success and fulfilment in life. Success is getting up one more time than you fall down. Don't dwell on the negative things, the problems - they will always be there. But dwell on the positive things.

Did you hear about the two positive thinkers in the army guardhouse? One said to the other,

"How long are you in for?"

"Thirty days."

"What did you do?"

"I was A.W.O.L. What are you in for?"

"Three days."

"What did you do?"

"I murdered the general."

"How come I get thirty days for being A.W.O.L. and you only get three days for murdering the general?"

"They're hanging me on Wednesday!"

There is always something positive in every situation that you find yourself in. The problem is that most of us don't want to see it. The best things in life don't come easy. They may come free, but not easy! Look for the positive things in life and not the negative.

No matter how hard the road ahead seems to be keep pressing on. Always dream and shoot higher than you know you can reach. Don't bother just to be better than your contemporaries and predecessors, try to be better than yourself.

Give me the man who says, "This one thing I do", not, "These fifty things I dabble in".

Never sacrifice depth for area.

Keep your eyes fixed on where you are going. Don't look at the detours and don't be distracted. In life keep seeing it big and keeping it simple.

A salesman passed the corner each day and after a week he began to pity the boy who was striving to sell his puppy. The salesman knew that the boy didn't see it big. He stopped and said,

"Son, do you really want to sell this dog?"

The boy replied, *"I certainly do."*

"Well, you're never going to sell him unless you learn to see it big. What I mean is - take this dog home, clean him up, doll him up, raise your price, make people think that they are getting something big and you will sell him."

That noon the salesman came by and there was the boy with the puppy now groomed, perfumed, with a ribbon around its neck and, alongside, a big sign:

"TREEEMENNDOUS PUPPY FOR SALE -$5,000".

The salesman gulped and realised that he had forgotten to tell the boy to keep it simple.

That evening he stopped by to tell the boy the other half of the formula only to discover that the boy was

gone, the puppy was gone and the sign lay there -
"SOLD" - written across it in big letters. The salesman
couldn't believe it. This kid couldn't have sold a dog
for $5,000! His curiosity got the better of him and he
rang the boy's doorbell. The boy came to the door
and the salesman said,

*"Son, you didn't really sell that dog for $5,000 did
you?"*

The boy replied, *"Yes, sir, I did and I want to thank
you for your help."*

The salesman said, *"How in the world did you do it?"*

The boy replied, *"Oh, it was easy. I just took two
$2,500 cats in exchange!"*

It's a well-known but good formula to have in life - see it
big, keep it simple. But, like any other formula, it is not
going to work unless you work.

I often feel that those who take the long road, the tourist
road, the long way around, do so because they lack
motivation in their lives.

Motivation comes largely from success breeding success.
If you go off onto tangents and zig-zag through life you
will lose the motivation and the sense of achievement that
you need to keep you going.

Here are some keys to keep your motivation and momentum going.

1. Learn to get excited about your work

I know that everything that we do demands details, monotony, preparation, striving, weariness - that's what we all have to overcome not matter what our work is. Learn to get excited about <u>your</u> work, not somebody else's. Develop a sense of importance and urgency in whatever you are doing.

A sense of urgency in your work informs you that yesterday has gone forever and tomorrow may never come, but today is in your hands. It lets you know that shirking today's work will add to tomorrow's burdens. It helps you accomplish the tasks that today sets before you.

Learn to get excited about what you are doing. It will put that sparkle into your life.

2. Always remember - what you don't use you lose

All of us must play the hand that we have been dealt. Finding out your talents and abilities is a lifelong process. Find out what you are good at and work on those skills. They are the raw materials from which you shape your destiny.

If you want to reach the top rank in anything you must feel good about your chances of success. The three most important things are - attitude, attitude and attitude. You are in this life to win not to lose. So - win!

How do you do it?

>   Firstly, know which battles you have to win
>   Realise that no-one wins all the time. Every sportsman knows that. Choose the things that you must win with care. Concentrate on the essentials and plot your course. Don't be distracted by friends, enemies or your own emotions.
>
>   Secondly, love to win
>   Don't concentrate on losing but love to win.
>
>   Thirdly, be relentless
>   Don't be sidetracked, no matter what happens.
>
>   By taking the long road you are only cheating yourself.

I heard about a young contractor who married a contractor's daughter and he had to learn the hard way. The father-in-law wanted to give a boost to his new son-in-law.

"Son", he said, "I don't want you to start at the bottom where I did. So I want you to go out and build the most tremendous house this town has ever seen. Put the best of everything in it. Make it a palace and turn it over to me."

Well, this was an opportunity to make a killing. He hurried out to slap together a building that would survive two fairly stiff gales. In short order he was back to his dear old dad.

"Well, dad, it's finished."

"Is it tremendous? Is it a palace like I asked?"

"Yes sirree, Dad."

"Is it the finest house ever built, son?"

"Yes sirree, Dad."

"All right. Where is the bill? Is there a good profit in it for you?"

"Yes, Dad, you bet."

"Very good. Here is your cheque and where is the deed?"

As he looked at the deed the father said, *"I didn't tell you why I wanted that house to be the best house ever built. I wanted to do something special for you and my daughter to show you how much I love you. Here, take the deed. Go live in the house - you've built it for yourself."*

The young man crept out a shattered, frustrated man. He thought that he was making a fortune at his father-in-law's expense by saving money on inferior materials and shortcuts, but he had cheated only himself. If you're tempted to take the long way around, the easy way, you are only going to cheat yourself.

Don't be distracted by the side roads. Keep that motivation going. Have clearly defined goals in your life. Don't lose your vision and your dreams. Select friends who will encourage you in the goals that you want to achieve in life.

Read books that will motivate you. Read the biographies of others that have achieved in life. Use your precious spare time when travelling, or when you are alone, listening to good tapes that will encourage you as well. Look for people who can serve to be mentors in life, people who have achieved, people who haven't left the track.

Hey, take a look at what is coming along down the highway. It's another one of those signs. Look - "The Tourist Route". It's the long way around. What are you going to do? Are you going to go off on a tangent, or are you going to keep on the highway, rolling down the road to success.

The choice is always yours.

Watch neglect.

Ivan Albright painted a picture, now hanging in the Chicago Art Institute, of an eight foot door, shaped like the lid of an old casket. The door is scarred and bruised, supposedly by the difficult experiences of life. A funeral wreath of wilted flowers hangs on the closed doors. The colours are dull and sombre. The painting is entitled, "That which I should have done I did not do". What a sad thought.

Undeveloped talent evaporates. Unused muscles atrophy. Undisturbed water pollutes. Unstirred air stagnates. Unwound clocks stop. Unentered doors close.

Neglect will ruin you.

The road marked
"TOMORROW"
leads to the town called
"NEVER"

NEGLECTING LITTLE THINGS

"In a career you either go forward or backward; you don't stand still. Every manager must continually improve his or her skills in a lifetime self-improvement programme.

- Mary Kay Ash

It is often the small things in life that cause us to stop and not reach our ultimate destinations and goals in life. Maybe as you started out on the journey you failed to check your tyres, maybe the battery was faulty, maybe there wasn't enough oil or it hadn't been changed. It's the simple little things in life that can stop us from achieving our ultimate goals.

It is true that the key to success is attention to detail. We must be careful to watch the little things in life.

The story is told about the American President, McKinley. It illustrates this point well. He was in a dilemma. He had to choose one of two equally capable men for a high diplomatic post. Both were old friends and he reminisced and recalled an incident that helped him to make his decision.

One stormy night McKinley had boarded a street car and had taken the last available seat towards the rear when an old washerwoman climbed aboard with a heavy basket of clothes. She stood in the aisle. Despite her age and forlorn appearance no-one offered her a seat. One of McKinley's two candidates, then much younger, was seated near her. He was immersed in a newspaper and took care to remain immersed in it so that he could ignore the old woman. McKinley went down the aisle, picked up the basket and led the woman to his seat. The man never looked up, never knew what had happened, nor did he ever know that this act of minor selfishness later deprived him of an embassy - the crown of his ambition.

The old song says, "Little things mean a lot" and they certainly do.

A well-known French chef said one time, *"Without sharp knives I am just another cook."*

It's those little things that make all the difference.

The leader keeps his finger even on the little things. He knows that whatever they may be, if they are mishandled they become big problems.

Oscar Hammerstein II once saw a close-up of the Statue of Liberty taken from a helicopter. The head of the statue was revealed in fine detail and Hammerstein noticed that the sculptor had done a painstaking job on the lady's hair. Every strand of hair was in its proper place. In his day the sculptor could hardly have known that anyone, save a possible seagull, would ever see that hair. But he gave it as much care as if it had been the face, the arm or the torch.

Michael Angelo painted the matchless frescoes on the high ceiling of the Sistine Chapel, spending countless hours on his back on the high scaffolding, carefully perfecting the details of each figure. A friend asked him why he took such pains with figures which could be seen only at a distance by viewers. *"After all"*, said the friend, *"who would know whether it was perfect or not?"* *"I would"*, replied the artist.

The "Old Faithful" in Yellowstone National Park gets its name from the fact that, unlike other geysers, it follows a dependable time schedule. Once every 65 minutes it shoots a stream of boiling water over 170' into the air.

Our lives ought to be characterised by faithfulness and dependability and that comes through making sure that we don't neglect the little things in life. The key to success is attention to detail.

It's the little things in life that add up to the big things. Termites destroy more property than do earthquakes. More fires are caused by matches and cigarettes than by volcanoes. One broken wheel can ditch a train. One quarrelsome worker can create a strike of ten thousand men. One vote can decide an election. One undiplomatic word can provoke a war involving thousands of lives and destruction of millions of dollars in property. One false step can cause a life or ruin a character. It is the neglecting of little things and the overlooking of small things that often stop us from reaching the goals that we want in life.

It is common knowledge that Alexander Graeme Bell invented the telephone. What is not so well-known is that, long before Bell's world-changing invention, a German schoolteacher by the name of Reis almost built the telephone. Mr Reis's phone would carry the sound of whistling or humming but would not transmit the human voice. Something seemed to be missing. Many years later Mr Bell discovered what that was. A little screw which controlled the electrodes on Mr Reis's invention, needed an adjustment of 1/1000th of an inch. Mr Bell discovered this error, turned the screw 1/1000th of an inch and was able to transmit speech loud and clear.

Now the telephone is considered as a household necessity. This infinitesimal distance of 1/1000th of an inch made a world of difference - the difference between failure and success. Mr Reis was very near success, yet he did not achieve it.

You see, the big shots in life are the small shots who just keep on shooting.

Benjamin Franklin used to say, *"For want of a nail the shoe was lost, for want of a shoe the horse was lost, for want of a horse the rider was lost, then overtaken and slain by the enemy. All for the want and care of a horseshoe nail."*

When the suspension bridge across the Niagara was to be erected the question was how to get the cable over. With a favoured wind a kite was elevated which alighted on the other shore. To its insignificant string a cord was attached which was drawn over, then a rope, then a larger rope, then a cable strong enough to sustain the iron cable which supported the bridge, over which heavily laden trains pass in safety.

Don't neglect the little things in life. Great men have often come from small beginnings. You see it is not where we start in life, it is where we finish.

Columbus was the son of a weaver. Oliver Cromwell was the son of a London brewer. Daniel Defoe was the son of a butcher. The great George Whitefield was the son of a innkeeper. Shakespeare was the son of a wood stapler. Abraham Lincoln was the son of a rail splitter.

Napoleon stood 42nd in his class at the military academy. But whoever heard of the other 41?

Henry Ward Beecher, as a boy, was a poor writer, a miserable speller, with a thick utterance and a bashful reticence which people mistook for stupidity. Booker T Washington was born a slave and became one of the most valued educators of his time. Michael Faraday, the greatest philosopher of his time, started from a blacksmith's anvil. It doesn't matter where we start only where we finish. The mighty Amazon begins as a mere icy trickle from an Andes glacier. As we do small things well so we will be entrusted with even greater things in life.

Whatever you are doing at the moment, no matter how small, do it as well as you possibly can. And the key is to get excited about what you are doing.

A doctor had a sign on his desk which said, "There is not much wrong with people that can't be cured by a little excitement".

Choose to keep moving down that highway. That's the important thing. Make sure you have attended to all the small things - the small details - in life. And then get moving. Don't sit around. It has been well said, *"Sitting and waiting won't put fish on the plate. The Lord provides the fishing, we have to dig the bait"*. You see we have to do something. The old saying is true - "If it is to be it is up to me".

We have choices. We have the freedom to make them. It doesn't matter where you are in life, what you are doing -

no matter how small. You have to develop creative genius. The world is just waiting for people who will use their creative genius.

You may have heard about the young boy who was waiting in a long line for a job interview. As the interviewer's secretary was going by he said to her, *"I want you to deliver this very urgent message to your boss"*. The secretary thought to herself, *"My, if it is that urgent I had better take it."* So she carried the note right into her boss's office. When she gave it to him he read it and began to laugh. The paper said, *"I am the 21st boy in line out here. Don't do a thing until you get to me"*! You can guess who got the job!

Don't neglect the little things in life. **Firstly**, everyone can be physically attractive. From your neck up you show the world what you think of the world. From your neck down you show the world what you think of yourself. Work hard on your personal presentation.

Secondly, work at being emotionally stable. People don't put their confidence in other people who are up and down like a yo-yo.

Thirdly, work at being intellectually awake. Don't be a couch potato. Keep filling your mind with those things which stimulate you intellectually. Read, study, discover more about the world in which you live. Every day is filled with possibilities.

Fourthly, be financially intelligent. Learn how to use your resources to the best possible advantage.

Don't neglect the little things in life. It is the attention to the small things in life that will take you on to greater things. It doesn't matter where we are in life we still have to give attention to the small things in life.

A reporter once asked Walt Disney how it felt to be a celebrity. *"It feels fine"*, he replied, *"when being a celebrity helps me to get a choice reservation for a football game. As far as I can remember being a celebrity has never helped me to make a good picture, or a good shot at a polo game, or command the obedience of my daughter, or impress my wife. It doesn't help me to keep fleas off our dogs and if being a celebrity won't give me an advantage over a couple of fleas, then I guess there can't be that much in being a celebrity after all."*

You see it's the little things in life that help us to really achieve greater things. Not giving attention to the small things in life can be one of the greatest detours that you will make in not achieving the goals that you want to achieve in life.

QUITTING TOO SOON

I am sure that you know what it is like to drive down a highway when it has been a long day. It has been a long drive and you see a sign flashing up there ahead which says,

"MOTEL - GOOD ROOMS FOR THE NIGHT"

It is so very easy to say, *"Well, I'll just pull over for a while, I'll just take it easy for a while, I'm tired, I don't think I can go on. I deserve a break."* So many have done this and not really achieved the things that they can in life.

Be very, very careful of this detour. It's so easy to go into a comfort zone rather than go on with the fight and achieve the things that you want to in life.

I read the story of Rafael Solano who sat on a boulder in the dry river bed, discouraged and physically exhausted and made an announcement to his two companions - *"I am through. There's no use going on any longer. See this pebble - it makes about 999,999 I've picked up and not a diamond so far. If I pick up another it will be a million. So what's the use? I'm quitting."*

It was 1942. The three men had spent three months prospecting for diamonds in a Venezuelan watercourse. They had worked, stooping, gathering pebbles, wishing and hoping for one sign of a diamond. Their clothes were ragged, their sombreros tattered, they had never thought seriously of quitting until Solano said he was through. Glumly one of them said, *"Pick up another and make it a million"*. *"All right"*, said Solano and stopped, put his hand on a pile of pebbles and pulled one forth. It was almost the size of a hen's egg. *"Here it is"*, he said, *"the last one"*. But it was heavy, too heavy. He looked. *"Boys, it's a diamond!"* he shouted.

Harry Wilson, a New York jewel dealer, paid Rafael Solano $200,000 for that millionth pebble. Named "The Liberator", it was the largest and purest diamond ever found.

Men don't fail, they give up trying.

Lord Nelson, England's famous naval hero, suffered from seasickness throughout his entire life. Yet the man who had destroyed Napoleon's fleet did not let illness interfere with his career. He not only learned to live with his personal weakness but he also conquered it. Most of us have our own little seasickness too. For some it may be physical, for others psychological. Usually it is a private war carried on quietly within us. No one will pin a medal on us for winning it but nothing can dim the satisfaction of knowing that we did not surrender.

Often it is not the wrong start but the wrong stop that makes the difference between success and failure. To quit while we are ahead would be silly. To quit when we are behind is even sillier. The trouble with most of us is that we stop trying in trying times. Few people travel the road of success without a puncture or two. It is always too soon to quit. If you encounter difficulty don't change your decision to go but change your direction to get there.

An eminent plastic surgeon told of a boy who lost his hand at the wrist. When he asked the lad about his handicap the boy replied, "I don't have a handicap. I just don't have a right hand." The surgeon went on to discover that this boy was one of the leading scorers on his high school football team. It's not what you have lost but what you have left that counts.

Failure is the path of least resistance. A problem is really an opportunity for a solution. Why and how a person comes up with a solution usually has to do with fresh eyes. Always try to look at a problem as if it were for the first time. Forget the ways that it has been handled in the past. Take nothing for granted except the assumption that a solution can be found. Try to get into a area of work that you enjoy doing.

An executive was asked one time about retiring. He responded, *"Why should I retire? Most people retire to do something that they have wanted to do all their lives. I'm already doing that!"* We quit easily because we lose the vision of what we really want to accomplish in life.

Failure should be our teacher not our undertaker. Failure is delay, not defeat. It is a temporary detour not a dead-end street. A winner is big enough to admit his mistakes, smart enough to profit from them and strong enough to correct them.

If you are facing obstacles in life it may be good for you to get some good advice. Here are some key steps in doing so:

Firstly, to get good advice - admit you need it. This is a humbling procedure but it means you are on the right track. It means that you have identified a problem and are prepared to correct it. It also means that you are prepared to listen.

Secondly, consider the source. Your best sources of advice are people who have no axe to grind and nothing to gain by offering you their counsel. You don't have to worry about hidden agendas or ulterior motives with these advisors. You don't have to ask, "Why is this person telling me this?"

<u>Thirdly</u>, go to the right source. You can never have too
many smart people in your life. What you need to do is:
 - identify the problem;
 - find an expert who can help;
 - don't be shy about asking him or her.

If you need good advice don't expect it to fall out of the
sky. Seek it out conscientiously, consistently and
aggressively.

<u>Fourthly</u>, build and maintain an informal board of advisors.
The President has his cabinet. You need people whom
you can turn to in different areas to help you in solving
problems and difficulties. Turning to people for counsel,
whether they are doctors or clergymen or lawyers,
accountants, mechanics, fitness instructors or hairdressers,
is the highest compliment that you can pay them. It
indicates that you respect them, trust them and think that
they are wise.

Get good advice as often as you can. Don't quit too soon.
Be persistent in what you are doing.

The bee has been aptly described as busy. To produce
one pound of honey the bee must visit 56,000 clover heads.
Since each head has 60 flower tubes - a total of 3 million,
360 thousand visits are necessary to give us that pound of
honey for the breakfast table. Meanwhile that worker bee
has flown the equivalent of 3 times around the world. To
produce one tablespoon of honey for our toast the little

bee makes 4,200 trips to flowers. It makes about ten trips a day to the fields, each trip lasting 20 minutes average and 400 flowers. A worker bee will fly as far as 8 miles if he cannot find a nectar flow that is nearer. Therefore, when you feel that persistence is a difficult task think of the bee. Persistence pays off in the long run.

Plato wrote the first sentence of his famous republic nine different ways before he was satisfied.

Cicero practised speaking before friends every day for 30 years to perfect his elocution.

Noel Webster laboured 36 years writing his dictionary.

Gibbons spent 26 years on his "Decline & Fall of the Roman Empire".

Sir Isaac Newton seldom went to bed before 2.00a.m.

Beethoven hardly wrote a bar of music that was not written and re-written at least a dozen times.

Leonardo da Vinci worked on "The Last Supper" for ten years. Often so absorbed he forgot to eat for whole days.

George Stevenson spent 15 years to perfect the locomotive.

Watts worked for 30 years on the condensing engine and

hard rubber cost Goodyear ten years of study, poverty and public ridicule.

"Work", declared Thomas A Edison, *"is mentioned not by hours but by what is accomplished."* Edison always kept a clock without hands on his desk. He believed that rewarding toil called for 2% inspiration and 98% perspiration!

There aren't any hard and fast rules for getting ahead in the world, just hard ones. An old Japanese proverb says, "There is no poverty that can overtake diligence".

Remember, by perseverance the snail reached the ark! A great writer said one time, *"It took me 15 years to discover I had no talent for writing, but I couldn't give it up because, by that time, I was too famous."*

George Bernard Shaw said, *"When I was a young man I observed that 9 out of 10 things I did were failures. I didn't want to be a failure so I did 10 times more work."*

Remember in the movie "Chariots of Fire", young Harold Abrahams - a champion sprinter - had just suffered his first ever defeat. After the race he sat alone, pouting in the empty grandstand. When his girlfriend tried to encourage him he bellowed, *"If I can't win I won't run!"*, to which she wisely replied, *"If you don't run you can't win!"* Abrahams went on to win the 1924 Olympic gold medal in the 100 metre run.

Many years ago in England there was a small boy who talked with a lisp. While growing up he was never a scholar. When war came along they rejected him with the comment *"We need men!"* He once rose to address the House of Commons and they all walked out. He often spoke to empty chairs and echoes. One day he became Prime Minister of Great Britain and led his country to victory in a world-wide conflict. That man was Sir Winston Churchill whose iron will to persevere rallied all his countrymen to defend their land and, eventually, win the war.

Here is the biography of a failure:

A man who had less than three years of formal education failed in business in '31, was defeated for the Legislature in '32, again failed in business in '33. He was elected to the Legislature in '34, defeated for Speaker in '38, defeated for Congress in '43. He was elected to Congress in '46 and defeated in '48, defeated for Senate in '55, defeated for the Vice-Presidential nomination in '56, defeated for the Senate in '58. His name - Abraham Lincoln.

"Always bear in mind that your own resolution to succeed is more important than any one thing."
- Abraham Lincoln

Rocky, the motion picture that won 3 Academy Awards, tells the story of a small-time boxer given the opportunity of a lifetime - the chance to fight the undisputed world heavyweight boxing champion. After weeks of punishing, gruelling training, on the evening of the fight Rocky finally admitted the futility of his efforts. *"Who am I trying to kid?"*, he pondered. *"I'm not gonna get in da same class wi' dat guy, but I gotta go da distance."*

Rocky Balboa set, as his goal, to go all 15 rounds. He wanted to hang in there when he knew that every muscle in his body would scream to quit. He wanted to endure under pressure. As a fighter he wanted to go the whole distance.

The fight began. But in round 1 Rocky was knocked down. The count commenced but, after wildly shaking his head back and forth, he struggled to his feet and mastered not just one or two more rounds but all 15. He was able to go the distance because, during training, his body had been subjected to gruelling preparation. Daily he had driven himself to the point of exhaustion - one arm push-ups, back bending sit-ups, sprinting, sparring - all this had been part of his schedule of training. The design of a demanding training schedule had enabled Rocky to endure.

Perseverance in any great test comes as a result of discipline and preparation in the ordinary days.

A teenager had decided to quit high school saying he was fed up with it all. His father was trying to convince him to stay with it.

"Son", he said, *"you just can't quit. All the people who are remembered in history didn't quit. Abe Lincoln - he didn't quit; Thomas Edison - he didn't quit; Douglas MacArthur - he didn't quit; Elmo McCringle ..."*.

"Who?", the son burst in. *"Who is Elmo McCringle?"*

The father replied, *"You don't remember him! He quit!"*

It is reported that Lord Wellington, after the great victory won over Napoleon at Waterloo, said, *"Our men were not braver than the enemy, they were brave five minutes longer."*

Today's opportunities erase yesterday's failures.

- Gene Brown

So you are driving down the highway and here comes that inviting sign -

"COMFORTABLE MOTEL AHEAD"

What is going to be your decision? Are you going to quit? Are you going to pull off? Or are you going to persevere and go through to achieve the goals that you want in life?

IF YOU WANT THE RAINBOW YOU HAVE TO ENDURE THE RAIN!

Chapter
9

THE BURDEN OF THE PAST

This next detour is one you must avoid at all costs. I call it "The burden of the past".

It is as though you are driving along the highway and you're towing a very heavy trailer. This is all the excess baggage from your past. Maybe they are discouraging memories - the memory of pain, of loss or of previous failure. We carry all these like heavy weights. It is easier to lie on a couch digging into the past than to sit on a chair facing the future. It is even harder to get up and walk forward.

Preoccupation with the past is always a retreat.

Be careful with those memories of the past. They can trap you in mud and make you incapable of moving forward.

David Livingstone, the great explorer, once explained, *"I will go anywhere as long as it is forward."*

Remember that life is growth and ceasing to grow by fearing the new will deny life. Nothing happens to you that hasn't happened to someone else.

Our past mistakes, as well as worthwhile accomplishments, are like a car's rear view mirror. While driving we use the broad view through the windshield as we move ahead but we also use the mirror for reference, making quick periodic glances into it for information to aid in making driving decisions. Although we cannot effectively, or safely, move ahead by staring only into the mirror, and ignoring the view from the windshield, proper use of the mirror does ensure a safer, smoother trip to our destination. In the same way we are not to dwell in our past but live by using the lessons of the past as a reference to aid our journey into the future.

You may have experienced failure and defeat in life. One of the greatest and most comforting truths is that when one door closes another door opens. But often we look so long and regretfully on the closed door that we do not see the one that has opened for us. Defeat is nothing but education. It is the first step towards something better.

At a coastal acquarium a savage barracuda quickly tried to attack the mackerel but was stopped by the partition. After bumping his nose repeatedly he finally quit trying. Later the partition was removed but the barracuda would swim only to the point where the barrier had been and stop. He thought it was still there. Many people are like that. They move forward until they reach an imaginary barrier but then stop because of a self-imposed attitude of limitation.

Emptiness is one of the greatest problems of our day. Too many people are looking to the past instead of to the future. It has been well said that, *"when goals go, meaning goes. When meaning goes, purpose goes. When purpose goes, life goes dead on our hands."*

You have got to <u>be</u> and <u>do</u> before you can <u>have</u>. If you are always looking to the past with all its failures and problems, then you are never going to achieve the things that you want to in the future.

I doubt whether there has ever been a person living who hasn't had regrets about things that have happened in the past. The choice that we have is - are we going to carry that heavy baggage with us into the future?

Omar Khyam once wrote, *"The moving finger writes and having writ moves on. Nor all thy piety nor wit nor all thy tears can cancel half a line of it."*

That trailer that you are pulling is just getting too heavy. It's time to pull to the side of the road and make a deliberate decision to uncouple the trailer and be free from it. Make the decision right now to be free from the past and to be ready for the future.

For too long now you have been writing yourself off. It may be your past background, or your level of education. Maybe it is the defeats or the discouragements that you have had in life. Maybe it is the family that you have come from. You have just been carrying too much excess baggage. Any athlete knows that to really be successful in the race they have to strip down to the bare essentials, they can't wear heavy coats and they certainly can't wear big, heavy boots if they want to win the race.

You are very different now from the infant that you were. You came into the world with nothing but through the years you have allowed yourself to be weighed down by so much heavy luggage that your journey through life has become a punishment instead of a pleasure.

The true worth of man is measured by the objects he refuses to pursue or acquire. The great blessings of life are already within you or within your reach. Carrying excess baggage - the burdens and problems, the failures of the past - will only rob you of love, peace of mind, happiness and the fulfillment of your goals.

As John Denver used to sing, "Some days are diamonds, some days are stone." You have been carrying these stones as weights for too long. It's time to off-load them.

Don't allow the problems of the past ruin your potential for the future.

Feeling sorry for yourself and your present condition is not only a waste of energy but the worst habit you could possibly have.

Stop living in the past. It's time to live in the present and start looking to the future.

COUNT YOUR BLESSINGS

Would you sell your eyes for a billion dollars? What would you take for your two legs? Your hands? Your hearing? Your children? Your family? Add up your assets, your are a billionaire.

> *I had the blues because I had no shoes;*
> *Until upon the street I met a man who had no feet.*

There are seeds of self-destruction in all of us that will bear only unhappiness if allowed to grow.

There are multitudes on this planet who have "blown it". How many have you heard of who have failed yet have stood up again, brushed off the dust and gone on?

Being tied to the memory of past failings can become a habit. The chains of habit are generally too small to be felt until they are too strong to be broken. But break them we must.

Among the greatest of human tragedies are the wasted lives of those who fail after enjoying success and who lose their desire to ever try again.

So you have failed - welcome to the human race! Are you going to allow the painful memories of the past to spoil the glorious opportunities waiting for you in the future?

The bee sucks honey out of the most bitter flowers.

The question is - do you really want to achieve those goals? Do you really want to do something with your life? Maybe there is a comfort zone in remembering the past failings. Maybe you would sooner be there than going into the unknown of the future. Maybe you want to be a martyr and carry those heavy burdens through life.

The time has come to free yourself from the memory of pain, of loss or of previous failures.

The time has come to disconnect that trailer that is just too heavy to pull along.

The time has come to be free from the past and to seize the future.

Lighten your load, beginning today.

Chapter
10

THE ILLUSION OF SUCCESS

This is for the person who thinks that they have arrived in life and this, too, is a deadly detour.

This is the person who plateau's in life, who ceases to strive, who doesn't want to go on to accomplish other great things in life.

These people feel that further accomplishment is unnecessary. They believe that they "have arrived", they don a mask and accept the high popular opinion of themselves.

Napoleon once said, *"The most dangerous moment comes with victory"*.

A man can do everything with a sword but sit on it. The same is true of success. Success is a journey not a destination.

The road to success is always under construction.

You must not say you have arrived, you must not plateau in life.

If you have achieved your dreams then dream bigger dreams.

You are probably amazed at how far you have come in life because you have set goals and now you are starting to achieve them. This is not the time to stop. This is the time to realise greater potential in your life.

Here are three key things to do.

> <u>Firstly</u>, learn and visualise clearly how other higher achievers think and act.

> <u>Secondly</u>, develop the characteristics of those high achievers.

> <u>Thirdly</u>, put into practice what you know and how it works.

In reality in life, if we are not going forward we are going backwards. That is why it is so important to dream some new dreams, to set time aside to gain some new visions, to set some fresh challenging goals.

What keeps you awake at night? What excites you? What new worlds do you want to conquer?

In his book "Man's Search for Meaning", Victor Frankl argues that the "loss of hope and courage can have a deadly effect on man". As a result of his experiences in a Nazi concentration camp Frankl contended that when a man no longer possesses a motive for living, no future to look toward to, he curls up in a corner and dies. *"Any attempt to restore man's inner strength in camp",* he wrote, *"had first to succeed in showing him some future goal".*

Some years ago a hydro-electric dam was to be built across a valley in New England. The people in a small town in the valley were to be re-located because the town itself would be submerged when the dam was finished. During the time between the decision to build the dam and its completion the buildings in town, which previously had been kept up nicely, fell into disrepair. Instead of being a pretty little town it became an eyesore. When did this happen? The answer is simple. As one resident said, *"Where there is no faith in the future there is no work in the present."*

It does not matter what we have achieved in life we must press on to even greater goals in the future. There is no telling the potential of your life if you are willing to develop it 110%.

Watch carefully this detour - the illusion of success.

Remember what the mother whale said to her baby: *"It's when you go to the top and start spouting that you get harpooned"*!

No one has fully arrived in this world.

On Abraham Lincoln's birthday an interesting cartoon appeared in a newspaper. It showed a small log cabin at the top of the mountain and the White House at the top of the mountain. A ladder connected the two buildings. At the bottom of the cartoon were the words: *"The ladder is still there."*

One of the most important lessons in life is that success must continually be won and is never finally achieved. Success is never permanent. The same is also true of failure.

Keep going. Don't stop. Keep climbing.

The secret of success is to be like a duck - smooth and unruffled on top but paddling like crazy underneath! The world expects results. Don't tell others about the labour pains. Show them the baby! The world is not interested in the storms you encountered but did you bring in the ship?

I notice you have just set the cruise control but it is too low. It's time to step up the momentum again. The speed of the leader determines the rate of the pack.

The biggest lament of top achievers is that they set their goals too low.

Remember the road to success is always under construction.

Chapter
11

GREEN LIGHTS FOR SUCCESS

We have been talking about some negative things - detours to stop you succeeding. Let's take a moment now to look at some green lights, some positive things that can help you to achieve real success in life.

1.   Do it now!

If you are at the traffic lights and the lights turn green, there is no sense in just sitting there. Even if you are on the right track you will get run over if you just sit there! You must constantly make the decision to do it now. Procrastination will cause you defeat in the future. If there is a phone call that must be made - do it now; a visit to make - do it now; a presentation to give - do it now; a letter to write - do it now. You will never succeed in life just by thinking about things. The key is to do it now.

"Waste your money and you're only out of money. But waste your time and you've lost a part of your life."
- Dr Michael LeBoeuf

2.   Organisation and appearance

Start to get your life organised. Start to plan your diary. Get your life organised so that you can achieve your goals. Take stock. Stop. Analyse. Find out what is necessary to get better organisation in your life. We go through life in such a muddle no wonder we don't achieve the things that we want to. There is so much crisis management. Life has enough upsets as it is. Nothing in life is going to go according to plan. That's the way life is - it is in constant movement. That is why it is doubly important to organise as much as we possibly can. You never know quite what the next telephone call will bring, what will happen during different times in your day. That is why it is crucial to bring organisation into your life.

And with organisation we must also work on our appearance. Our appearance speaks volumes of what we want to do and achieve with our lives. To build that better dream you must build a better you. Make your appearance an asset. To act right you have to look right and feel right. Be well-groomed. Make your appearance an asset not a liability. You only have one chance at a good first impression. And it is to your advantage to make a good first impression. If you are well-dressed it adds to your self confidence.

How do you know what to wear? The key is appropriateness. You wouldn't wear what you wear to the beach for a business meeting. Read up on dress in a good book. Shop around. Clothes needn't cost the earth but make sure they are clean and pressed. Keep your shoes clean, polished and in good repair. Good grooming starts from the shoes up. Keep your nails clean and trimmed. If you wear them, keep your glasses clean. Study someone who has good dress sense. Perhaps he/she can help you with some good advice. How you carry yourself is so important as well. It conveys to people whether or not you are in charge of the situation, that you know where you are going.

3.   Be cheerful and optimistic

Positive anything is better than negative nothing. Of all the things you wear your expression is the most important. Keep on smiling - remember it only takes 13 muscles to smile, a frown costs 64! So it's more economical anyway! A smile is an inexpensive way to improve your looks. Rather than lowering your eyes the next time a stranger approaches you try this - look him or her squarely in the eyes, smile and say "hi".

When McDonalds was preparing to open its first outlet in Moscow the most difficult task for trainers was teaching their employees to smile. They had been grim for so long in the Soviet Union. It sounds simple doesn't it? Success by smiling - but it works and it is infectious. Most people are about as happy as they make up their minds to be. The happiness of your life depends on the quality of your thoughts. So be cheerful and optimistic and always remember - it is nice to be important but it is more important to be nice!

Dr G Campbell Morgan tells of a man whose shop had been burned in the great Chicago fire. He arrived at the ruins the next morning carrying a table. He set it up amid the charred debris and above it placed his optimistic sign, *"Everything lost except wife, children and hope. Business will be resumed as usual tomorrow morning."*

4.   Self-control

Carefully monitor your health. Remember you can't find success in the hospital. Maintain good health habits. To be really successful and effective you must keep yourself in good shape. So many successful people suffer with their health because they fail to discipline themselves. Take a trip to any shopping mall and observe the physical conditions of the people who parade by.

A flood of evidence has been produced to show that bad habits are detrimental to good health. But make sure that you keep everything in balance. Enjoy life - moderation is the key.

Here are a few areas you may need to keep constantly working on:

*   Exercise - that means playing some sort of sport or jogging or swimming just to keep you in shape.

*   Keep your weight down - minimise the amount of fat consumed in your diet.

* Don't use too much salt.
* Get regular sleep.
* Keep the caffeine intake down.

* Nutrition and diet - your body is in a constant state of change and needs good nourishment. Get some good advice on nutrition. Watch the overuse of sugars.

* Successful people, because they use up energy, need a well-balanced vitamin intake. Experiment and get some good advice as to what is good for you. You may need to invest in a regular medical check-up.

  Ensure recreation time is not overlooked. We need to be constantly re-created.

* Then, too, think on good things. Deliberately put out of your mind the unpleasant and ugly experiences of life and force yourself to think about pleasant and uplifting thoughts, the beauty around you, the good, the right, the beautiful.

* Watch your words. Keep your vocabulary positive.

Here are some suggestions:

Eliminate these words completely	Make these words a part of your vocabulary
1. I can't	1. I can
2. If	2. I will
3. Doubt	3. Expect the best
4. I don't think	4. I know
5. I don't have the time	5. I will make the time
6. Maybe	6. Positively
7. I'm afraid of	7. I am confident
8. I don't believe	8. I do believe
9. (minimise) I	9. (promote) You
10. It's impossible	10. It is possible

5. Say something nice to everyone you meet

Learn the habit of praising and encouraging other people. You will find it is like a boomerang - it will come back to you. People are crying out for encouragement in life. Give encouragement wherever you can. Give people hope for the future. Say things like - "you did a great job", "you are going to make it".

Lack of encouragement is the biggest cause of turnover in employment today. It is the reason why so many kids leave home, couples divorce and employees leave organisations. What they are really saying is - "they didn't really encourage me". I'm not talking about hype or false hope but genuine heartfelt encouragement. Help people realise their potential. Give them hope for the future. Show appreciation to them.

Say often:

- "Thank you";
- "I really appreciated the way you helped out" ;
- "Thanks for getting that job done so quickly"

Praise loudly, blame softly. Praise in public, discipline in private.

Constantly affirm people and encourage personal strengths. Remember to recognise people as well.

Be aware of your team's accomplishment - "You did a great job on that letter", "You are building a great team".

Your family, friends and team all need your love and encouragement. Few other strengths are as important to the successful person as that of building up others.

Every person deserves, and needs, to know how their leader feels about his or her performance. Build on their strengths. Imagine them in ten or twenty years' time. How can you develop their full potential?

Benjamin Disraeli said, *"The greatest good that you can do for another is not to just share your riches, but reveal to him his own."*

6. Make somebody like you

Here are some golden tips:

a)   Treat everyone you meet as if he or she is the most important person you will meet that day. Leave the impression with everyone that they are important to you. After a while there should be nothing phony or manipulative in this because these people will become important to you.

b)   Develop a great handshake. Don't grab a person's hand like a dead fish. Instantly you get the right message across with the right handshake, the right smile and the right attitude.

c)   Take a mental note of the colour of their eyes as you shake their hand. As you make this a habit it will not only force you to look into their eyes but also puts a twinkle in your eyes. It creates a special moment of interaction with the other person. Smile for a moment or two longer than they do.

d)   As you shake hands think of something positive about that person. They will sense the vibes more than you realise.

e)   Sincerely compliment people. People really do care what you think about them and they really do appreciate your praise.

f)   Learn to feel people's emotions and moods not what they are just saying. You need to flow with the other person's emotions and mood and identify with them. Empathise with them.

g)   Never lose the wonder. Develop that special ability to be genuinely interested in people and their special interests. Become fascinated in what they are and do.

Now here is something which may sound a little silly. I read it somewhere and it really works. Here it is - when you are talking with someone, simply use their name at the start and at the end of a sentence and make your request. You must tilt your head and smile a little as you say their name. Just give it a go - you have nothing to lose!

Above all, be sincere. Don't be phony or manipulative with people, they are all too precious for that.

The development of people skills will put you light years ahead.

7.   Enthusiasm
If you aren't fired up with enthusiasm you may well be fired - with enthusiasm! Enthusiasm is the fizz in the lemonade. Learn to be enthusiastic about all that you say and do. Get enthusiastic about the project that you are into at the moment.

"If you love your work you'll be out there everyday trying to do it the best you possibly can and pretty soon everybody around will catch the passion from you - like a fever."

- Sam Walton

8.   **Keep going**

Don't lose the dream, the vision and the goals. The one who lacks the courage to start has already finished.

A quitter never wins and a winner never quits.

People don't fail, they simply give up. So keep going. The green light is on. It's time to get moving.

9.   **Four all-important words**:

i)   **Dream** - keep the dream ahead of you all the time.

ii)   **Study** - study the area that you are involved in. Make sure that you know everything that you possibly can about it.

iii)   **Plan** - put your goals in writing. If you can't put it on paper you probably can't do it. 97% of people in our society do not have an organised goals programme.

Thoreau said, *"If one advances confidently in the direction of their dreams they will meet with success unexpected in common hours. "* If you build castles in the air your work will be lost. That is where they should be. Now put your foundations under them. Put your plan - your goals - into action.

Why is that most people don't have an organised goals programme?

The first reason that most people do not have a goals programme is fear. They are afraid of the future - of what may, or may not, happen.

Secondly, people do not have a goals programme because that they have a poor self-image.

The third reason is because they have never completely understood the benefits.

The fourth reason is that 97% of people who do not have a goals programme do not know exactly how to develop the programme.

iv) **Action** - you can have all the dreams, all the visions and all the plans but you have got to put them into action. Develop a plan of action for your life and stick with it.

"Give me a stock clerk with a goal and I will give you a man who will make history. Give me a man without a goal and I will give you a stock clerk."   J C Penney

It is time now to practically and systematically set out your goals. Remember, goals are a set of specific, measurable steps that design the programme for fulfilling your vision.

A.   Make a list of your goals.

Write down all the goals that you can think of in the four areas: being, doing, owning, accomplishing. Start with 20 years, then 15, then 10, then 5, then 1 year, then 6 months, then 90 days, then 60 days.

B.   Now rearrange them in order of priority for each of the four areas. Select the goals you want first. Next set a target date. Be realistic. Make them attainable goals. A goal without a deadline is not really a goal - it is a wish.

C.   Make a list of the required action you must take to achieve your goal. For example, the extra effort required, or more study, or the cash needed. (Remember - no gain without pain.)

D.   Develop the qualities in your personal behaviour that will be required. Obtain the skills. For example - a pleasant personality, neat appearance, mental awareness, a winning smile, a warm handshake, a positive walk or plain hard work.

E.   List your deficiencies and conquer them, starting right now! Today!

F.   List the personnel or help needed to achieve your goals and the techniques or methods as well.

G.   Develop an iron will determination to follow through your plans regardless of obstacles, criticism or circumstances, or what other people say, think or do.

H.   Visualise the new you. Vividly imagine yourself as having already reached your goals.

I.   Begin at once.

In the absence of clearly defined goals we are forced to concentrate on activity and, ultimately, become enslaved by it. Remember, there is no joy in victory without running the risk of defeat.

OPPORTUNITIES NEVER COME TO THOSE WHO WAIT, THEY ARE CAPTURED BY THOSE WHO DARE TO ATTACK.

The fulfillment of our goals must be good for others. If they bring harm to others then our goals are selfish. The great rewards in life are love and achievement. All else is secondary. Become a giver, not a getter. Don't be afraid to set goals.

The great football coach, Vince Lombardi, said one time, *"The price of success is hard work, dedication to the job at hand and the determination that, whether we win or lose, we have applied the best of ourselves to the task at hand."*

To achieve goals demands hard work, determination and commitment. For many, though, the main reason they do not establish a quest to achieve goals is plain fear; the fear of ridicule from others or the fear of defeat. Others fear that their goals will not be perfect - or, worse still, they may consider themselves presumptuous.

The importance and the benefit of goalsetting is immeasurable. Without setting goals your visions and dreams are just wishful thinking. There are so many benefits in goalsetting. They make decision making easier. Your physical and mental health is better. You have established a positive attitude to life. You are helping to eliminate stress, confusion and fear. Those who have goals attract respect from people. It give you a sense of accomplishment. It gives you "stickability" and staying power. It is staying power that sets the leader apart.

THE TRAGEDY OF LIFE DOESN'T LIE IN NOT REACHING YOUR GOAL; THE TRAGEDY LIES IN HAVING NO GOAL TO REACH.

Henry Kaiser said, "Determine what you want more than anything else in life, write down the means by which you intend to attain it, and permit nothing to deter you from pursuing it".

Without goals and priorities we will never escape the tyranny of the urgent. If we do not have our eyes fixed on a goal the urgent will crowd out the important. Goalsetting accomplishes your vision.

"After the cheers have died and the stadium is empty. After the headlines have been written and after you are back in the quiet of your own room and the superbowl ring has been placed on the dresser and all the pomp and fanfare has faded - the enduring things that are left are:
- the dedication to excellence
- the dedication to victory
- the dedication to doing with our lives the very best that we can to make the world a better placed in which to live."   Vince Lombardi

I hope that you have determined in your mind to stay on the highway to success, that you won't take any of the detours, that you will take all the green lights and you will go forward to become truly successful with your life.

Remember - the past is great, the present is wonderful, but the best is yet to come. Let's get into overdrive.

Make your future your friend.

May you live all the days of your life.

I AM A BUSINESS BUILDER

- *I BRING TOGETHER IDEALS AND PEOPLE*

- *I ORGANISE TALENTS AND RESOURCES*

- *I DEVELOP OPPORTUNITIES THAT EXPAND THE HUMAN POTENTIAL*

- *I MAKE DREAMS A REALITY*

- *I AM A SURVIVOR, OVERCOMING OBSTACLES EVERY MINUTE OF EVERY DAY, LEARNING FROM EACH FAILURE AND GROWING STRONGER WITH EACH SUCCESS*

- *I AM A BUILDER BY HARD WORK, LOYALTY, HONESTY AND DETERMINATION, I AM A DOER, A DREAMER, AND AN OPPORTUNITY CREATOR*

- *I AM A BUSINESS BUILDER*

OTHER BEST SELLING BOOKS BY BILL NEWMAN:

1. THE TEN LAWS OF LEADERSHIP

Just as there are principles that govern nature, so there are definite principles which are vital in leadership. Don't stagger on in ignorance. Study well these principles to become the leader you are meant to be.

2. TEN EXCITING KEYS TO SUCCESS

No one wants to climb the ladder of success only to find the the ladder is leaning against the wrong wall! Success is a series of right choices. Here are the exciting keys to success - principles that have proven so effective in the lives of so many - just waiting to be proven in yours.

3. STRAIGHT TALK TO YOUTH

Is especially designed for our teenagers as they become Christians. Not "do's" and "don'ts" but life principles on the subjects of "Real Love", "Real Friendship", "Finding a life-long partner", "Living Victoriously".

4. FAMILY LIFE IN THE FAST LANE

The needs of families have never been greater than today. Bill Newman gives you some sensible keys for strengthening and enriching marriage and family life.

5. SOARING WITH EAGLES

Eagles are magnificent creatures. Since ancient times many have used the eagle as their symbol and for good reason, as this exciting book will show. These principles of success are vital to us all. Allow the monarch of the skies, the eagle, to teach you how your life can count.